SPIRITUALITY

...He Who Is Spiritual...
I Corinthians 2:15

Stephen Kaung

ISBN: 978-1-942521-38-9

Available from:

Christian Testimony Ministry
4424 Huguenot Road
Richmond, Virginia 23235

www.christiantestimonyministry.com

Printed in USA

CONTENTS

During the weekend of October 7-10, 1994, Stephen Kaung shared at the seventh Northeast Christian Weekend Conference at Harvey Cedars Bible Conference, Long Beach Island, New Jersey. The theme of the conference was He Who Is Spiritual, during which time brother Kaung shared two messages on Spirituality, followed by a question and answer period.

What is true spirituality? What is real and what is counterfeit? Through these mes-sages, Stephen Kaung provides answers to these questions as revealed by the word of God.

The spoken word has been transcribed and edited for clarity. Unless otherwise indi-cated, Scripture quotations are from the New Translation by J. N. Darby.

SPIRITUALITY: TRUE AND FALSE

I Corinthians 2:15—But the spiritual discerns all things, and he is discerned of no one.

Matthew 23:1-33—Then Jesus spoke to the crowds and to his disciples, saying, The scribes and the Pharisees have set themselves down in Moses' seat: all things therefore, whatever they may tell you, do and keep. But do not after their works, for they say and do not, but bind burdens heavy and hard to bear, and lay them on the shoulders of men, but will not move them with their finger. And all their works they do to be seen of men: for they make broad their phylacteries and enlarge the borders of their garments, and love the chief place in feasts and the first seats in the synagogues, and salutations in the market-places, and to be called of men, Rabbi, Rabbi. But ye, be not ye called Rabbi; for one is your instructor, and all ye are brethren. And call not any one your father upon the earth; for one is your Father, he who is in the heavens. Neither be called instructors, for one is your instructor, the

Christ. But the greatest of you shall be your servant. And whoever shall exalt himself shall be humbled, and whoever shall humble himself shall be exalted.

But woe unto you, scribes and Pharisees, hypocrites, for ye shut up the kingdom of the heavens before men; for ye do not enter, nor do ye suffer those that are entering to go in. Woe to you, scribes and Pharisees, hypocrites, for ye compass the sea and the dry land to make one proselyte, and when he is become such, ye make him twofold more the son of hell than yourselves. Woe to you, blind guides, who say, Whosoever shall swear by the temple, it is nothing; but whosoever shall swear by the gold of the temple, he is a debtor. Fools and blind, for which is greater, the gold, or the temple which sanctifies the gold? And, Whosoever shall swear by the altar, it is nothing; but whosoever shall swear by the gift that is upon it is a debtor. Fools and blind ones, for which is greater, the gift, or the altar which sanctifies the gift? He therefore that swears by the altar swears by it and by all things that are upon it. And he that swears by the temple swears by it and by him that dwells in it. And he that swears by heaven swears by the throne of God and by him that sits upon it. Woe to you, scribes and Pharisees, hypocrites, for ye pay tithes of mint and anise and cummin, and ye have left aside the weightier matters of the law, judgment and mercy and faith: these ye ought to have done and not have left those aside. Blind guides, who strain out the gnat, but drink down the camel. Woe to you, scribes and Pharisees, hypocrites, for ye make clean the outside of the cup and of the dish, but within they are full of rapine and intemperance. Blind Pharisee, make clean first the inside of the cup and of the dish, that their outside also may become clean. Woe to you, scribes and Pharisees, hypocrites, for ye are like whited sepulchres, which appear beautiful outwardly, but within are full of dead men's bones and all uncleanness. Thus also ye, outwardly ye appear righteous to men, but within are full of hypocrisy and lawlessness. Woe to you, scribes and Pharisees, hypocrites, for ye build the sepulchres of the prophets and adorn the tombs of the just, and ye say, If we had been in the days of our fathers we would not have been partakers with them in the blood of the prophets. So that ye bear witness of yourselves that ye are sons of those who slew the prophets: and ye, fill ye *up the measure of your fathers. Serpents, off-spring of vipers, how should ye escape the judgment of hell?*

Matthew 5:1-12—But seeing the crowds, he [our Lord Jesus] went up into the mountain, and having sat down, his disciples came to him; and, having opened his mouth, he taught them, saying, Blessed are the poor in spirit, for theirs is the kingdom of the heavens. Blessed they that mourn, for they shall be comforted. Blessed the meek, for they shall inherit the earth. Blessed they who hunger and thirst after righteousness, for they shall be filled. Blessed the merciful, for they shall find mercy. Blessed the pure in heart, for they shall see God. Blessed the peace-makers, for they shall be called sons of God. Blessed they who are persecuted on account of righteousness, for theirs is the kingdom of the heavens. Blessed are ye when they may reproach and persecute you, and say every wicked thing against you, lying, for my sake. Rejoice and exult, for your reward is great in the heavens; for thus have they persecuted the prophets who were before you.

Let us have a word of prayer:

Lord, as we come into Thy presence and as we are before Thy word, we do tremble. We acknowledge, Lord, that Thy words are life and spirit. We pray, Lord, that Thy Holy Spirit will quicken Thy words to our hearts; that they may not be just the letter that kills but the Spirit that quickens. Lord, we do acknowledge that we are completely at Thy mercy. We ask in Thy precious name. Amen.

Thank God for bringing us together. The theme of this time together is the spiritual, in other words, true spirituality. In the past, we have considered together a number of spiritual truths. We have talked about spiritual vision. How important it is that we have vision! We have talked about spiritual responsibility. Each one of us is responsible for what the Lord has called us to and given to us. We also talked about spiritual ministry. We are not only to minister unto our brothers and sisters as Levites, but we need to minister to the Lord as priests. We have also mentioned spiritual authority, how important it is, because without spiritual authority, there can be no building of the house of God. Together with it, of course, there is spiritual submission, which is required of everyone. Submit to one another in the fear of Christ. Also, we talked about the spiritual house, how we need to be built up together into a spiritual house, the holy habitation of God in the Spirit.

All these truths can only be operative among spiritual men and women. If we are not spiritual, then none of these spiritual truths will be effective or workable. So the first thing that is needed is that we be spiritual in the sight of God. You know, we all want to be spiritual and, in a sense, I am afraid we try to appear to be more spiritual than we really are. It may not be our intention but, unconsciously, probably every one of us is in such danger. That is the reason why we need to consider very seriously before the Lord this matter of spirituality: false or true.

THE SCRIBES AND PHARISEES

Our Lord Jesus came to this world to bless, and yet you find at one time He proclaimed "woes" to a certain class of people. In Matthew 23, seven times our Lord Jesus proclaimed "woes" to the scribes and Pharisees. He called them hypocrites, fools, blind. Seven times—in verses 13, 15, 16, 23, 25, 27, 29—you find our Lord Jesus proclaimed "woes" to the scribes and Pharisees. Why? Because they are hypocrites. They are acting; they are playing a part on the stage; they are not real. This is something to which our Lord Jesus is deadly opposed.

Who are these scribes and Pharisees? In Matthew 23, you will find they were a people who seated themselves in Moses' seat. They considered themselves the disciples of Moses and, as a matter of fact, they even sat in Moses' seat. They were not only those who studied the law, they were not only those who claimed that they kept the law, but they were even those who became interpreters of the law. They decided what was lawful and what was unlawful. They considered themselves the teachers of all, and yet, they put burdens upon people's shoulders but they themselves would not even lift a finger.

The Lord said, "You may listen to what they say, but do not do what they do because they do not do the things that they teach. They are hypocrites." Do they do anything? Yes, they do. But what they do is all for the sake of being seen and praised by man. They broaden their phylacteries and enlarge the borders of their garments to show how pious they are. Instead of keeping the law in their heart, they put it on their forehead. They put it on their garment to show that they are a godly people. They love the first seat in the synagogues. They love to be called, "Rabbi, Rabbi." Now the word *Rabbi* means "the great one." They are the great ones. They not only consider themselves Rabbi, but even father; not only father, but even instructor, guide. They consider themselves the guides of all the innocent people. They are not the instructed, they are the instructors. Now these are the people upon whom our Lord proclaimed His woes.

FALSE VERSUS TRUE SPIRITUALITY

Pride Versus Poor In Spirit

Woe unto you, scribes and Pharisees, hypocrites, for ye shut up the kingdom of the heavens before men; for ye do not enter, nor do ye suffer those that are entering to go in. (Matthew 23:13)

The first woe was proclaimed to these scribes and Pharisees because they stood in the way of the kingdom of God. They did not enter in themselves; and even when people were entering in, they forbade them to do so. How did they do it? Well, they considered themselves *the* teachers, *the* interpreters; they considered themselves as those who were "in the know." They knew everything, and because they thought they knew everything, therefore, their pride kept them away from the kingdom of God.

When John the Baptist came and said, "Repent, for the kingdom of the heavens has drawn nigh," they rejected him because they thought they had nothing of which to repent. They might have needed some improvement, but they had no need to repent in such a drastic way as to be baptized, that is, to bury the past as if there was nothing good of the past and to have to start all over again. They thought they were too good for that. They considered themselves *the* orthodox; they were the mainline, the religious. Because of that, their pride kept them away from the kingdom of God, and their jealousy kept people who were going in from entering in. That was their situation.

It is just the opposite of what the Lord said on that Mount in Matthew 5. The first beatitude says, "Blessed [happy] are the poor in spirit, for theirs is the kingdom of the heavens." The poor in spirit! It is not "poor spirit," it is "poor in spirit." Why are they poor in spirit? It is because they know they are nothing. They know nothing; they acknowledge their spiritual poverty, and with that kind of attitude, the kingdom of the heavens is theirs. So, they are the very opposite of the scribes and Pharisees.

Now, brothers and sisters, are we poor in spirit or do we think of ourselves as the orthodox ones? "We know everything and we are right, only *we* are right." If we have that kind of attitude, we are hypocrites. This is false spirituality. In Christianity today, there are more scribes and Pharisees than we realize. I wonder if we ourselves are among the ranks. Are we sitting in Moses' seat? Do we think that we are the keeper, the guardian, the interpreter of the law of God? Are we telling people what they should do and yet, we ourselves do not do it? Are we seeking for the glory of man? to be seen? to be praised? to be called Rabbis, teachers? Is that our secret desire? Is there pride in our heart; do we think that we are the elite, we are the people who know? If that is the case, then, brothers and sisters, "Woe to the scribes and Pharisees." We are not entering into the kingdom of God and probably, our jealousy will keep people from going in. Orthodoxy can be dead orthodoxy.

Zeal For Tradition Versus Mourning And Repentance

Woe to you, scribes and Pharisees, hypocrites, for ye compass the sea and the dry land to make one proselyte, and when he is become such, ye make him twofold more the son of hell than yourselves. (Matthew 23:15)

The scribes and the Pharisees were very zealous. They would go to the end of the world to bring in one proselyte but, unfortunately, they did not really bring people to God. They brought people to their tradition, to their own system, and after they got people into their tradition, into their system, they made them even worse than themselves.

In the beatitudes, it says, "Blessed are they that mourn, for they shall be comforted." Who are the mourning ones? They refer to people who mourn over their sinfulness, mourn over their weaknesses; they know they are not what they should be, and because they have such an attitude, they shall be comforted. In Isaiah, it says that the heaven and the heavens cannot contain our God but He will abide with the afflicted and the contrite in heart and those who tremble at His word. Again, you find these scribes and Pharisees the opposite of the mournful ones because they were so confident of themselves and they were zealous for their tradition. They did not have that right attitude before God.

Brothers and sisters, is it possible that maybe we also are very zealous? For what are we zealous? Are we really zealous for the Lord and for His interest, for His kingdom, or are we just zealous for our tradition, for our religious system? You find that many people will fight for their tradition, but they will not fight for the name of the Lord; they are religious fanatics. Are we such people? Or do we maintain a constant spirit of repentance before the Lord? I do believe that repentance is not just to be done once in a lifetime. I believe repentance is a spirit, an attitude that we need to keep every day before the Lord. Otherwise, we can easily become a religious fanatic. "Woe to the scribes and the Pharisees, hypocrites."

Carnally Minded Versus Spiritually Minded

Woe to you, blind guides, who say, Whosoever shall swear by the temple, it is nothing; but whosoever shall swear by the gold of the temple, he is a debtor. Fools and blind, for which is greater, the gold, or the temple which sanctifies the gold? (Matthew 23:16-17)

This is the third woe that our Lord proclaimed over these people. Is that not strange to your ears when you hear that they said, "Well, if you swear by the temple, it is nothing"? The temple was where the Lord put His name; it was the dwelling place of God. But they said, "No, if you swear by the temple, it is nothing; but if you swear by the gold of the temple, then you are a debtor." That was their teaching. You can see their mind-set from what they taught. They were not spiritually minded at all. They did not really see what the temple was. Their mind was on the gold. The gold was more important than the temple. The gold meant much more to them than the temple itself. In the same way, they said, "If you swear by the altar, it is nothing; but whosoever shall swear by the gift that is upon it is a debtor." The Lord said, "Which is greater, the altar that sanctifies the gift, or the gift?"

So, you can see that their mind was a reprobate mind. They looked at material things as more important than spiritual things. They looked at man's effort—humanistic—more than what is from God. Yet, they taught it as if it were *the* teaching. So, the Lord said, "You are fools, you are blind."

Now in the beatitudes, the Lord said, "Blessed are the meek." Who are the meek? To put it simply, the meek are the teachable. The meek are those people who know that they know nothing. They know very little, and they are teachable, they are humble—low and meek in their heart. But the very opposite of meekness is this attitude of self-importance, self-assurance, self-confidence; and they teach people as law. Such blindness!

Brothers and sisters, what is our condition? Are we spiritually minded or are we carnally minded? If we are carnally minded, our teaching will be in the same manner as that of the scribes and the Pharisees. You may think it is ridiculous: How could you consider the gold as more important than the temple? But, brothers and sisters, many are teaching in the same tenor.

Legalism Versus Practical Righteousness

Woe to you, scribes and Pharisees, hypocrites, for ye pay tithes of mint and anise and cummin, and ye have left aside the weightier matters of the law, judgment and mercy and faith: these ye ought to have done and not have left those aside. Blind guides, who strain out the gnat, but drink down the camel. (Matthew 23:23-24)

These scribes and Pharisees were very careful in paying their tithes: one-tenth of mint, anise, and cummin, even those very small things. They were very careful to give one-tenth to the Lord. And yet, the Lord said that there were weightier matters of the law that they completely neglected: judgment, mercy, and faith. In other words, they were very legalistic. They were the most legalistic people in the whole world. They kept to the very small letter of the law, and they missed the whole spirit of the law.

In the beatitudes, the Lord said, "Blessed are they who hunger and thirst after righteousness, for they shall be satisfied." In other words, are we hungry for righteousness? It is not only Christ as our righteousness. When we come to our Lord Jesus as a sinner, He clothes us with the best robe, that is, Himself as our righteousness. But the righteousness in the beatitudes is more than that. Not only do we take Christ as our righteousness, but we seek after practical righteousness. In other words, because He is righteous, therefore, we must be righteous— righteous in our everyday life, righteous as the result of Christ being incorporated into our very being. We seek for righteousness.

But these scribes and Pharisees did not seek for righteousness, they just sought for an outward thing. They paid one-tenth of anise, cummin, mint, these physical things and, yet, they neglected the real thing. So, they were hypocrites. They were blind.

Dear brothers and sisters, where are we? Are we legalistic or are we spiritual? The Lord Jesus said, "Unless your righteousness exceeds the righteousness of the scribes and Pharisees, ye cannot enter into the kingdom of the heavens." The righteousness of the scribes and Pharisees is just a facade, an outward thing, but they do not have the real righteousness within them. How easily we can fall into the same trap.

External Appearance Versus Internal Reality

Woe to you, scribes and Pharisees, hypocrites, for ye make clean the outside of the cup and of the dish, but within they are full of rapine and in-temperance. Blind Pharisee, make clean first the inside of the cup and of the dish, that their outside also may become clean. (Matthew 23:25-26)

To put it in one word, they were very careful about the external appearance, but they neglected the inward goodness. They washed the outside of the cup, but the inside was full of rapine and intemperance. That was what they were—everything was just external. There was no internal realness in their lives.

In the beatitudes, the Lord said, "Blessed are the merciful, for they shall receive mercy." We who have received the mercy of God need to be merciful. Mercy is an inward quality. The Lord said, "God does not love sacrifice, He loves mercy." Those who only look after the outward appearance, the external things and not the inward reality are hypocrites. To put it another way, they are those who are pseudo-spiritual— not really spiritual, but who pretend to be spiritual.

The Form Of Godliness Versus Life Within

Woe to you, scribes and Pharisees, hypocrites, for ye are like whited sepulchres, which appear beautiful outwardly, but within are full of dead men's bones and all uncleanness. Thus also ye, outwardly ye appear righteous to men, but within are full of hypocrisy and lawlessness. (Matthew 23:27-28)

They whitewashed the tombs, but within the tombs were those rotten bones. In other words, they had the form of godliness but without the power of it. The Lord said, "Blessed are the pure in heart, for they shall see God." Who are the pure in heart? They are single-minded towards God, and because they are pure in heart, they see God. By seeing God, they are being transformed from glory to glory and conformed to the image of God's Son, Jesus Christ, by the Spirit of God. These are the true, spiritual ones. But people who only attend to the form of godliness and do not have the power of godliness, that is, the life within them, are of false spirituality.

Offspring Of Vipers Versus Sons Of God

Woe to you, scribes and Pharisees, hypocrites, for ye build the sepulchres of the prophets and adorn the tombs of the just, and ye say, If we had been in the days of our fathers we would not have been partakers with them in the blood of the prophets. So that ye bear witness of yourselves that ye are sons of those who slew the prophets:

and ye, fill ye up the measure of your fathers. (Matthew 23:29-32)

These scribes and Pharisees built the tombs of the martyrs, repaired the tombs of the just, thinking, "If we were there, we would not have done these things." But the Lord turned it around and said, "This proves that you are the sons of those who killed the prophets, and as a matter of fact, you fill up the cup of their sin."

"Blessed are the peace-makers, for they are sons of God." Those who are not only at peace with God but who bring peace among God's people, who bring peace to the world are sons of God. Even though these scribes and Pharisees tried to build the sepulchres of the prophets, they were the very ones who persecuted and killed the prophets and they even wanted to kill the Savior, our Lord Jesus. These scribes and Pharisees were hypocrites, pseudo-spiritual; they had a false spirituality—and what a class they were! Finally, the Lord proclaimed His judgment over them. He said, "Serpents, offspring of vipers, how should ye escape the judgment of hell?"

Even though our Lord Jesus proclaimed woes to these scribes and Pharisees, He did not do it out of hatred but out of love. Yes, He was angry at their pretensions; His Spirit was stirred by their hypocrisy. Yet, our Lord Jesus did not proclaim these woes to them out of hatred. He spoke the truth in love, hopeful that light might come upon some of the scribes and Pharisees, that they would turn away from their false spirituality and become really spiritual. That was the intention of our Lord Jesus.

PUT YOURSELF UNDER GOD'S LIGHT

So, brothers and sisters, we need to be searched by God's light. The psalmist said, "In Thy light we shall see light." If we surround ourselves with the light that we ourselves kindle, we will lie down in sorrow because we are deceiving ourselves. I know that as we read Matthew 23 and as we are fellowshiping on it, it seems that there is a kind of heaviness there. It is heavy but, brothers and sisters, we need to be honest. We need to put ourselves under this light; we need to be willing to expose ourselves under the light of God, even these seven-fold woes in Matthew 23. We need to put ourselves under this light. It is not that we try to examine ourselves because self-examination, self-introspection only gets us into a worse situation; but we put ourselves under the light of God's word and let His light search us out to see if there is any pretension, any deception in our lives, to see if we think more highly of ourselves than we actually are. Sometimes, people look at us as being higher than we really are or lower than we really are. That is the people's judgment. But whatever it may be, we need to put ourselves under the light of God, under His word and let His word examine us, search us, prove us. If there is anything that His word would touch, repent, because that is the reason the Lord put these words before us.

Thank God, if there is a counterfeit, there is bound to be a genuine thing. In this world, there are so many counterfeits but, thank God, there are genuine things in this world, too. The same thing is true in Christianity today. There is so much pseudo-spirituality; it is everywhere, but we know this only proves there is true spirituality. So that is what we are going into.

MAN IS CREATED SPIRIT, SOUL, AND BODY

Heathen Philosophy Versus Christian Truth

It is the will of God for His children to be spiritual. God is Spirit. He wants every child of His to be spiritual. Remember, He wants us to be spiritual, but He does not want us to be spirits. We have a false concept. We think that to be spiritual, we have to be spirits, like the angels. The angels are spirits. We think this body is evil: if we could only get rid of this body, then we could be spiritual. If we could only get rid of this soul and become soulless, then we could become spiritual. It is this body and it is the soul that are evil. They keep us from being spiritual. So, we want to get rid of it in order to be spiritual. Remember, this is heathen philosophy; this is not Christian truth. In heathen philosophy, whether it is eastern or western, the body itself is considered as evil. So, the way to overcome evil is to get rid of this body. If you can get rid of this body, then you are home free. In heathen philosophy, the evil is the soul. If you can be reduced to being a soulless person—you think not, you feel not, you will not—then you arrive at Nirvana; you are complete, you are spiritual. That is false. That is heathen philosophy. That is not Christian truth.

God created us with a spirit, a soul, and a body. God created us with a spirit that we may commune with Him, the Spirit. God created us with a soul that we may think, we may feel, we may will. God created us with a body that we may touch, we may know what is around us. This is God's creation, and it is the will of God and the divine order that our spirit should be at the top as the master of the being. Our spirit is in touch with the Spirit of God and, then, our soul is the steward. It will receive from the spirit God's will, God's order, and it will pass it down to our body, which is the servant to act, to carry it out. Now this is the divine order.

The Fall—Spirit Dead to God

Unfortunately, because of the fall of man, you will find that our spirit is dead towards God. In Genesis, God said, "On the day that you eat of the forbidden tree, you shall surely die." Adam and Eve ate the forbidden fruit but, physically, they continued for hundreds of years. They begot sons and daughters. They were very much alive physically and soulically, but their spirit was dead on the day they ate of that forbidden tree. In other words, it was not that the spirit was not there—they still had the spirit—but the spirit was dead so far as God is concerned.

The scientific definition of death is "the cessation of communication with its proper environment." That is death. Your body communicates with the physical world, but when your body ceases to communicate with the physical world, that is death. Your spirit's proper environment is God. When you cease to communicate with your proper environment, God, your spirit is dead. The organ is still there, but it has lost its function towards God; how-ever, it has not lost its function towards the spirit world.

At the fall of man, our human spirit became dead to God, so the soul and the body are left and are active. Man has become flesh. Flesh is the combination of the soul and the body without the spirit. Sin enters into man and dwells in the body, so the body becomes the body of sin and of death. It has become the body of sin because it can do nothing but sin. It has become the body of death because it cannot do what it should do, so it is death. The soul is so contaminated by sin that the self-life which dwells in the soul is a selfish, corrupted, sinful self. It is not that the body itself is evil; it is indwelt by sin that is evil. It is not that the soul itself is evil; it is created by God. It is the fallen self as the life of the soul that is evil. So, brothers and sisters, we need to be delivered. First of all, our spirit needs to be quickened into new life. Then, our soul needs to have self dethroned and Christ enthroned. Then, our body needs to be delivered from being an instrument of unrighteousness and of sin into being an instrument of righteousness unto God.

You know, people today are dealing with the symptoms. They do not deal with the source. Trying to get rid of the body does not solve the problem. Trying to be soulless does not solve the problem. You need to have your spirit quickened, your soul sanctified, and your body delivered. That is where the salvation of the Lord comes in.

Quickening of the Dead Spirit

The first step towards true spirituality is the quickening of our dead spirit. If our dead spirit is not quickened, there is no possibility of being truly spiritual because spirituality begins in the spirit. Anything that does not begin from the spirit is a counterfeit; it is false spirituality. People may have beautiful, noble thoughts and ideas. People may see beauty in this universe. People may have very warm feelings and affections. People may have very strong determination and will. They may have a strong determination towards God. They may have a very warm feeling towards God. They may even have very noble, beautiful thoughts about God, but if it does not originate from the spirit, it is a substitute, a counterfeit. It is false spirituality.

Remember the story of Mary in Luke 1. She said, "My soul magnifies the Lord, and my spirit has rejoiced in God my Savior." It is true that her soul magnified the Lord. There was warm feeling towards the Lord, but where did this originate? Not from the mind, but from the spirit: "My spirit *has* rejoiced in God my Savior." So, anything that does not originate from the spirit but comes from the soul as its source—and some souls can really soar very high—is false spirituality. Anything that does not have its source from the spirit but from the body is false spirituality. You may be very energetic, you may have good plans, you may be very successful in Christian work, but that does not mean spirituality. It has to come from the spirit.

So, there is no possibility for people who are not born again to be truly spiritual—no possibility. The first step towards true spirituality is new birth. He that is born of the Spirit is spirit. He who is born of the Holy Spirit is the new spirit. Our spirit which was dead in sins and transgressions needs to be quickened into new life.

God said, "I will put a new spirit within you; and I will put My Spirit within your spirit to cause you to walk in My statutes, to keep My ordinances, that you may do them" (see Ezekiel 36:26-27). Brothers and sisters, this is the beginning of true spirituality. Unless you are born again, there is no possibility of being truly spiritual. How are you going to be born again?

You cannot do it yourself; but when you come to the Lord Jesus, confess your sins, accept Him as your Savior and Lord, the Holy Spirit will at that very moment touch your dead spirit and bring it to life. Immediately, your communication with your proper environment, God, will be resumed. You will cry out, "Abba, Father," and that will start you on the road to true spirituality.

The Holy Spirit—The Agent Of True Spirituality

Now, let me go a step further. Spirituality has to come from the spirit, but not everything that comes from even our renewed spirit is spiritual. We may think if it comes from the spirit, it has to be spiritual. No; it can be false, because, as a matter of fact, spirituality comes from the Holy Spirit. He is the agent of true spirituality. It is He who glorifies Christ; it is He who incorporates, builds Christ into your very life. The Holy Spirit is *the* agent of true spirituality. Thank God, He dwells in your spirit. Everyone who is born of the Spirit not only has a new spirit, but God said, "I will put *My* Spirit into your spirit." So, the Holy Spirit dwells in your spirit, bearing witness with you that you are the child of God. Thank God, the

Holy Spirit is there in you, and if your spirit is in tune with the Holy Spirit, listens to the Holy Spirit, obeys the Holy Spirit, receives from the Holy Spirit, is taught by the Holy Spirit, then what comes out of your spirit is true spirituality. Otherwise, it can come from the spirit, but if it is not from the Holy Spirit, it is a counterfeit.

In Luke 9, our Lord Jesus was on His way to Jerusalem. He set His face towards Jerusalem as the lamb going to be sacrificed. That was His Spirit. But as He passed through the Samaritan villages, those villages would not receive Him because He was traveling towards Jerusalem. They had such hostility against the Jews, they would not receive the Lord. The two Sons of Thunder, James and John, how they thundered! They said, "Lord, do You want us to call down fire from heaven to burn them up like Elijah did?" Oh, they had such faith! They believed if they called for fire, fire would come down and burn them up. They had such love and zeal for the Lord. They were all for the Lord. How could people not receive the Lord? Death is the only consequence! Remember what the Lord said: "You do not know what spirit you have." The

Lord's Spirit is the Spirit of the lamb going to be sacrificed, not the spirit of the lion going to devour. So, even what was coming out of the spirit of these two Sons of Thunder was not true spirituality. It was false spirituality, and it can do much harm. Why? Because our spirit can be invaded by our soul. When our spirit is invaded by our soul, even if it is good flesh, it contaminates; not only that, our spirit can also be invaded by the evil spirit. That is the reason why not everything that comes from the spirit is true spirituality. It has to come from a spirit that is in subjection to, in cooperation with the Holy Spirit who dwells within our spirit. Then you have true spirituality.

In II Corinthians 7:1, it says how we need to purify ourselves from the pollution of the flesh and the spirit, perfecting holiness in the fear of God. So, thank God, it is His will that we be spiritual, and He has opened a way for us to be truly spiritual. It begins with a reborn spirit, and as we learn to be in subjection to the Holy Spirit who dwells in us, then we are on the way to true spirituality.

Shall we pray:

Dear heavenly Father, we want to thank Thee that it is Thy will for us to be spiritual and Thou hast made every provision for us to be truly spiritual, to the praise of Thy glory. So, Lord, we pray that Thou will continue to examine us, bring us under the light, and open our understanding that we may really be delivered from all that is false and enter into that which is true that will glorify Thy name. We commit ourselves to Thee in the name of our Lord Jesus. Amen

WHAT IS TRUE SPIRITUALITY?

THE MARKS OF TRUE SPIRITUALITY

I Corinthians 2:15—But the spiritual discerns all things, and he is discerned of no one.

I Corinthians 15:45-46—Thus also it is written, The first man Adam became a living soul; the last Adam a quickening spirit. But that which is spiritual was not first, but that which is natural, then that which is spiritual.

II Corinthians 4:7—But we have this treasure in earthen vessels, that the surpassingness of the power may be of God, and not from us.

Philippians 1:21—For for me to live is Christ.

Philippians 2:5—For let this mind be in you which was also in Christ Jesus.

Philippians 3:10—...to know him, and the power of his resurrection, and the fellowship of his sufferings, being conformed to his death.

Philippians 4:13—I have strength for all things in him that gives me power.

Another translation says: I have strength for all things through him who empowers me.

Shall we have a word of prayer:

Dear Lord, our hearts are full that Thou dost love us so much and dost command us to remember Thee at Thy table. We do praise and thank Thee that Thou dost give Thyself to us. Lord, it is the desire of our heart that Thou will have us wholly for Thyself. Lord, on the one hand, we do long for Thy return that we may see Thee face to face; yet, on the other hand, we are fearful lest very little can really satisfy Thy heart. So, Lord, it is our prayer before Thee that Thou may increase in us and we may decrease. Do not allow us to live in a false condition. Lord, we want to be real. We want Thee to be all, and we trust Thy Holy Spirit to do such a work.

Lord, as we gather here this morning, we feel that the time is so short. Unless Thou dost a double work in us, Lord, how are we going to see Thee? We lay ourselves at Thy feet and invite Thee to perfect the good work that Thou hast begun in every one of us, to the praise of Thy glory. We commit this time into Thy hands. We acknowledge that this is something that Thou alone can do. We are helpless, and we just lean upon Thee. We ask in Thy precious name. Amen.

In our time together, we are burdened with this one thing: the spiritual. We realize that unless there is true spirituality, not only do we not really have anything, but the Lord will have very little; and it is our desire that the Lord will have much for Himself. He who loves us so much and gave His all to us deserves to have much from us. So this is our desire and the reason we have gathered together to consider this matter of true spirituality. It is really not just for ourselves; it is for Him.

Last time, we tried to draw a picture, a contrast between true and false spirituality: Matthew 5 really describes to us what is true spirituality, and Matthew 23 really tells us what is the counterfeit—false spirituality. In Matthew 5, after you go through the beatitudes—to the blessed—what is the impression that is left with you? I believe the impression that is left with you is Christ. Even though it says, "Blessed are the poor in spirit," yet, it is Christ that you see in the poor in spirit. When you read Matthew 23, what is the impression you get? With those who are cursed, you get the impression of religion.

On the one side, it is the living Christ in us—that is true spirituality. On the other side, it is being religious; it is the religious flesh, a counterfeit, a pretension, playing a part on the stage. There is nothing more dangerous for God's children or there is nothing more opposite to spirituality than "religiousity." We become very religious because, by being religious, we think we are spiritual. It is a substitute, a counterfeit, a deception. We may be very orthodox but dead; we may be very traditional but have no revelation; we may be very legalistic but have no life; we may have a form of godliness, but where is the power of it? We become divisive instead of peaceful. We see in Christianity today that this is the situation. We see such situations among God's people everywhere: "We are the orthodox; we have the truth; we know what is right." We become proud, jealous, but where is Christ? Where do we see Him?

Now we would like to fellowship together on true spirituality and the marks of true spirituality. In I Corinthians 15, it says that the first Adam was a living soul and the last Adam a quickening spirit. That which is natural comes first, and then that which is spiritual. I want to borrow these two verses. When you think of Adam, you think of the natural man. When you think of Christ, you think of the spiritual man. The natural man comes first and then the spiritual man. All that is of Adam is natural, and the natural man does not appreciate the things of the Spirit. It is something that is beyond him; he does not know of the things of the Spirit. Therefore, it is impossible for a natural man to be spiritual. If a natural man tries to be spiritual, it is pseudo-spirituality; it is a pretension.

We who have believed in the Lord Jesus, in a sense, are not classified among the natural man. We who are the Lord's, who have believed in the Lord Jesus, even though we do not belong to the natural man, yet, we can be classified as the carnal man. The only difference between the carnal man and the natural man is, the natural man is just soul and body without a spirit; the spirit is dead. The carnal man has his spirit quickened, renewed and, yet, he still lives according to the flesh and not according to the Spirit. The Bible says that he is a carnal man. A carnal man may know the things of the Spirit, but a carnal man cannot obey the Spirit. It is impossible for a carnal man to be spiritual. That carnality has to be dealt with before there is the possibility of being spiritual.

The Corinthian believers were carnal Christians. They were Christians, but they were carnal Christians, and for carnal Christians to pretend to be spiritual is a counterfeit. We want to make it very clear that spirituality is not possible to the natural man and spirituality is beyond the carnal man. God has to do something in our lives to bring us into true spirituality.

THE PATTERN OF TRUE SPIRITUALITY

What is spirituality? Who is the spiritual one? We already have said that Christ is the spiritual man. Of all men, Christ is *the* spiritual man. He is the spiritual man in his perfection. In both the Old and New Testaments, we find a number of people who are spiritual, but they are spiritual within measure. Our Lord Jesus is spiritual without measure. God has given Him the Holy Spirit without measure. So He is *the* pattern of true spirituality.

Most Human—Most Spiritual

Look at our Lord Jesus. Because our Lord Jesus is spiritual, is He therefore less human or inhuman? Probably, our concept is that if we are to be spiritual, we cannot be human; if we are not inhuman, at least we should be less human, then we become spiritual. That is a false concept because our Lord Jesus is the most perfect human being. He is the friend of sinners and publicans. He loves the children. He is accessible, approachable, open to all. He is holy and righteous and, yet, you do not have the feeling that He says, "I am holier than thou." He is merciful, gracious.

He was tempted in all things. Our Lord Jesus, while He was on earth, was tempted in any temptation that you can think of to which a human being could possibly be exposed. Do not think that you are tempted in anything in which our Lord has not been tempted. He was tempted in all things, yet without sin. He wept. He was distressed in His soul. At times, He was oppressed in His spirit. When He was rejected, He felt it; and yet, He rose above it. "Father, I thank Thee, Thou hast revealed Thy mind to the babes and closed it to those who consider themselves wise and prudent." Our Lord Jesus felt the pain, the suffering, the rejection. Think of Gethsemane. Think of Calvary. He was most human and, yet, most spiritual. He was spiritual not because He was human; He was human because He was spiritual.

Now to us, it is just the opposite. We need to be human before we can be spiritual. Think about this. If we are not human, we cannot be spiritual. By human, I do not mean fallen humanity, I mean the human being that God had in His mind when He created man.

A Life in the Spirit

The whole life of our Lord Jesus is one with the Spirit of God. Not only the Father and the Son are one, but the Son and the Spirit are one. In His last conversation with His disciples before His death, He said, "I will send you another Comforter and you know Him because He is with you and He shall be in you." Now, who was with the disciples at that time? The Lord Himself. Yet, the Lord said, "Another Comforter,"—because the Holy Spirit and the Lord are one—"He is with you and He shall be in you." That is, after our Lord Jesus died and was raised from the dead, then He was glorified and the Spirit was given. He is another comforter of the same kind, not of another kind; He is the same, just as our Lord.

He was born through the overshadowing of the Spirit of God upon the womb of the virgin Mary. After He was baptized, the heavens were opened and the Spirit of God descended like a dove upon Him; not only upon Him, but He took up His abode in Him. He was indwelt by the Spirit of God. When He came back from the temptation in the wilderness, He was full of the power of the Holy Spirit. When He began His ministry, He said that the Lord had anointed Him, the Spirit was upon Him." Throughout His life, you find He and the Holy Spirit are indivisible; they are one; in His life, in His ministry—one. It is by the eternal Spirit that He offered Himself once for all, spotless, to God as the sacrifice. Brothers and sisters, this is spirituality: a life in the Spirit.

Look at the life of our Lord Jesus. You will find that, throughout His life, He never lived for Himself. He lived *by* the Father. He said, "The Father has sent Me and I live on account of Him" (see John 6:57). In other words, He lived by the Father, not by Himself. He lived *for* the Father, not for Himself. He said, "I have glorified Thee and I have done the work Thou hast sent Me to do" (see John 17:4). He lived *in* the Father. He told Philip: "Have I been so long with you and you still ask to see the Father? Don't you know that I am in the Father and the Father is in Me?" (see John 14:9-10). So, here you find a man—He is spirituality in its perfection, very human and yet highly spiritual; this is our Lord Jesus. This is the pattern of true spirituality.

A Man In Christ

Let us consider the apostle Paul and how he learned of Christ in this area of spirituality. Paul is a man of like passion as we are. If Paul can be spiritual, then we too have hope. Who is Paul? He is a man in Christ. Paul said, "I know a man in Christ; fourteen years ago this man was raptured to the third heaven—whether in the body or out of the body, I don't know. I know a man in Christ; fourteen years ago he was caught away to paradise and heard things that can not be uttered. I know that man" (see II Corinthians 12:2-4). Now in reading it, you know that it is Paul himself. He is a man in Christ.

There are two books in the New Testament that reveal Paul, the man, and his ministry: II Corinthians and Philippians. If you want to use one word to write over I Corinthians, it is *carnality*. If you want to use one word to describe II Corinthians, it is *spirituality*. Even though II Corinthians is more of the description of the spiritual ministry of the apostle Paul, yet, we know that ministry and life cannot be separated. We could talk about II Corinthians from the viewpoint of spiritual ministry, and that is what it is; but we will borrow this book and use it to look at Paul as a man in Christ.

Second Corinthians opens with tribulations and sufferings. That is what life is. Paul was a man who knew tribulations and sufferings. Yet, on the other hand, you find that he knew the consolations of God. Unfortunately, many people know tribulations and sufferings, but they do not know the consolations of God. This man had the sentence of death upon his life. He said, "I despair of living," and yet, he knew the resurrection power of Christ.

This man had a desire to visit Corinth. He loved the Corinthian believers. He wanted to visit them and even give them a double visit. That was his desire, and he told them so; but circumstances changed, and he did not go. Then the people said, "Now, look at this man, he is not dependable." Paul said, "Yes, I changed my mind. I would rather be true than be consistent. But the gospel that I preach is not 'yea and nay.' In Christ, it is 'Yea and Amen.'"

We think this man was so strong and, yet, when he was in Troas, the door to the gospel was wide open, but he could not find Titus. Titus went to visit the Corinthians. Paul had a prearrangement with Titus, and he was waiting for him to bring back the news, but Titus was delayed. Titus was not there at Troas. Even though the door of the gospel was wide open, Paul could not work. So he left; he went to Macedonia. What a failure! Human. Yet, he said, "Thanks be unto God who always leads us in the triumph of Christ."

He was faithful to the Corinthians, and out of his faithfulness, he wrote a strong letter to them. That letter was lost—it was not I Corinthians. He wrote that letter with tears. He was so burdened for the Corinthians. He spoke the truth in love— a strong letter but with tears, many tears. After he wrote the letter, he felt uneasy about it: "Oh, why did I write such a letter? It was too strong." Yet, when the good news came, he was comforted. That letter had produced the right result. He was very human.

When he was rejected, he felt it very deeply and, yet he said, "The less I am loved, the more I will love you. I am willing to spend and be spent for you." Here was a man who was forced to be a fool and, yet, he was one who had visions and revelations; a man who had a thorn in his flesh and, yet, he knew the grace of God was sufficient for him.

Treasure in an Earthen Vessel

What do you see in that man? He was an earthen vessel but with a treasure in it. What is true spirituality? True spirituality is an earthen vessel with a treasure in it that the surpassingness of the power may be of God and not of man. In other words, it is the power of the treasure that comes through the earthen vessel. That is true spirituality. True spirituality is *not* the earthen vessel. We try to refine the earthen vessel, to decorate the earthen vessel, to make the earthen vessel look spiritual—but that is not it. Or we go to the other extreme and say, "Destroy the earthen vessel. It is such a hindrance. Oh, if I could only destroy that earthen vessel—no more human—then I would be spiritual." No. The earthen vessel must be there; the humanity is there. But there is no spirituality with the earthen vessel by itself; there must be treasure in the earthen vessel.

What is true spirituality? We say it is the treasure. No, if it is only the treasure without the earthen vessel, it is not true spirituality. That is what we have been saying. True spirituality is the divine life coming through humanity. That is true spirituality. It is a paradox. You will always feel weak; the earthen vessel is weak, fragile, easily crushed and cracked. It will always be there and, yet, Paul said, "I boast in my weakness because when I am weak, then I am strong." A paradox. It is Christ getting through a human life—that is spirituality. So, do not be too idealistic, thinking that it is all treasure and no earthen vessel. That is not what God wants, and you will never reach that point. It is treasure in the earthen vessel. You see the humanity in Paul—very human—and yet, through that humanity, you see Christ. That is true spirituality.

THE WAY TO TRUE SPIRITUALITY

Regeneration

If that is true spirituality, how do we get there? Let me put it very simply: the way to true spirituality, first of all, of course, has to begin with regeneration—new birth. Spirituality has its source in the Spirit and, thank God, when He "rebirths" us, quickens our dead spirit into life, He puts His own Spirit in us. The Holy Spirit is the sole agent of spirituality. Without Him, there can be no spirituality. Thank God, every child of God, every born-again person, not only has a new spirit but has the Holy Spirit dwelling in his spirit. The work of the Holy Spirit is to bring us into spirituality, to be the spiritual, because this is the will of God. God's will is not for you to be carnal, to be a babe all your life. God's will is for you to be a son or daughter of God. In Romans 8, He said, "He that is led by the Spirit is the son of God." So we need to be led by the Spirit, and that is what the indwelling Spirit is doing in our lives.

Consecration

How does it start? You have the new spirit; you have the Holy Spirit dwelling in your spirit. Everything is now ready on the road to spirituality; but the door needs to be opened, and the key is consecration—Romans 12. I was saved when I was fifteen. I sought the Lord for a whole year. The Lord evaded me; but after a whole year of seeking after Him, finally, He met me when I was ready to give up, and I told Him so. I told the Lord, "If You do not save me this time, bye bye," and He saved me that very afternoon. Thank God.

According to traditional Christianity, the last day of a convention or conference is always on consecration; and by consecration, it means to be a minister or a Bible woman or a missionary; that is the concept. A large map of China hung on the wall behind the platform, and the preacher was just pounding: "If you love the Lord, give yourself, consecrate yourself to Him and go and preach the gospel." He even told us: "You can choose where you want to go." I was a young man just saved, so grateful to the Lord. When the preacher said, "Come to the platform and point your finger to the place where you want to go," I thought, "In China, where is the most difficult place, the farthest place? Mongolia." So I went to the platform; I pointed my finger at Mongolia: "That is where I am going." I was serious, but even until now, I have never been to Mongolia.

What is consecration? Consecration is not doing something for God. Consecration is giving yourself to Him and letting Him do the work—that is consecration. He is going to do a great work in your life to make you spiritual, but He will not force you. He is waiting for you to open the door, to give Him permission. Think of that! He has every right over you, and He just waits for your permission. Consecration is offering, presenting your body a living sacrifice. It is saying, "Lord, I am here at Your disposal. Do what is upon Your heart." That opens the door for the Holy Spirit to begin to work in your life.

Christ Enthroned In Our Soul

Our soul needs to be sanctified. Who is dwelling in our soul? Self, you, me. We are saved by the grace of God; the work of grace has already begun in our spirit, but it has to reach out to the soul. Yet, you find our self is on the throne of our soul. This fallen self, this sinful self, this selfish self is in control of our soul life. He is expressing himself through our emotion; he is expressing himself through our mind, our thought life; he is expressing himself through our volition, our will. A transformation has to come so that our soul will express Christ and not ourselves. Or to put it another way: Christ has to be enthroned in our soul. Our self has to be displaced and replaced by Christ. That is what you find in Ephesians 3, in Paul's prayer: "That Christ may dwell in your heart." Christ dwells in your spirit today, but does He dwell in your heart? Do you allow Him to come and fill your heart, take charge of all your soul faculties and express Himself through you?

How does it come about? The Holy Spirit will arrange your environment. Remember, as a child of God, even our hairs are numbered; not only counted, but numbered. Every hair has a number, so when you combed your hair this morning, certain numbers fell, and God knows it. You do not know it, but God knows it. He loves us to such an extent. Do you think that your environment could be by chance, a coincidence? Never. As you give yourself to the Lord, He will arrange your circumstances, and through these circumstances, He is bringing in the cross for you to bear. Do not create your own crosses; it is the work of the Holy Spirit—there will be plenty.

51

Whether it is people or events or things or relationships, whatever it may be in your daily life, the Holy Spirit arranges your circumstances and He speaks within your spirit. He tells you to take up your cross and follow the Lord.

The Way Of The Cross

What is a cross? A cross is something that crosses your way. You want to go in one direction, and the Lord says, "No, it is the other direction." That is a cross. You want one thing, and the Lord says, "No, the other thing." That is the cross. You want the world, and the Lord says, "No, My will." That is a cross. The cross serves only one purpose: to crucify the self. That is why our Lord Jesus said, "Deny yourself, take up your cross and follow Me. Otherwise, you cannot be My disciple"; that is to say, "You will never learn."

Denying self is a matter of will. After you have given yourself to the Lord, then the will is there. Take up the cross. You have to do it. It is an active, positive thing; you can evade it, bypass it, but if you are willing to take up the cross so that your self will be crucified, done away with,

Christ will come in and take the rightful place. That is the reason Paul said, in II Corinthians 4, "We bear in our body the slaying of Jesus that the life of Jesus may be manifested in our mortal body." We are delivered unto death daily that we may know life daily. If we evade the cross, self will never be dethroned and Christ will never be enthroned in our heart and the transformation will not come. So it is very important: this way to spirituality is the way of the cross.

THE HOW OF TRUE SPIRITUALITY

I wonder if any of you have read Francis Schaeffer's *True Spirituality*. In that book, he said the "how" to true spirituality is not by human effort or energy. The how of true spirituality is actually Romans 6:11: "Reckon ye yourself"—that is faith—"dead unto sin in Christ"—that is the negative aspect—"and alive unto God in Christ"—that is the positive aspect. So, he said the how of true spirituality is simply this: the power of the crucified, resurrected, and glorified Christ Jesus through the agency of the Holy Spirit and by faith.

I remember J. N. Darby said, "True spirituality is not necessarily high intellectual understanding of the doctrines of the Scriptures. You find true spirituality in the most common believers whose all is Christ." True spirituality is Christ in you.

Philippians is the letter that reveals Paul, the spiritual man. In Philippians 1:21, he said, "For me to live is Christ." That is the meaning of true spirituality. You have the "me" there, you have Christ there; and it is not the "me" who lives, it is Christ who lives. For me to live, it is Christ who lives in me—that is true spirituality. You live, but it is not you who lives—it is a mystery—it is Christ who lives in you.

The sign of true spirituality is the mind of Christ— a mind of humility, a mind of emptying oneself, a mind of esteeming others as more excellent than you are, a mind of obedience. Those are the signs of true spirituality.

The way to true spirituality is in Philippians 3:10: "To know Him, and the power of His resurrection, and the fellowship of His sufferings, being conformed to His death."

The power of true spirituality is Philippians 4:13: "I can do all things through Him who empowers me." False spirituality says, "I can do all things;" but in John 15, the Lord says, "Apart from Me, you can do nothing." Have we come to that point yet: "Apart from Him, we can do nothing"? But you know, some brothers and sisters stop there. "I can do nothing. So, I do nothing." They become very passive. Well, this is the preparation. If you can do all things, then Christ can do nothing. So, you have to be brought to the point that you come to see that you can do nothing apart from Him, and then you realize "I can do all things through Him who empowers me." That is the power of true spirituality.

THE MARKS OF TRUE SPIRITUALITY

Poor In Spirit

What are the marks of true spirituality? I will just mention a few. First of all, I think the mark of true spirituality is being poor in spirit. "Blessed are the poor in spirit, for theirs is the kingdom of the heavens." Pseudo-spirituality is the spirit of the Laodiceans: "I am rich; I grow richer; I have need of nothing; I have everything." The Lord said, "You do not know you are wretched, miserable, poor, blind, naked." The Pharisee went into the temple and prayed, "God, I thank You because I am not like other people who are so sinful. Oh, I am not like that publican. I give tithes, one-tenth of everything; I fast twice a week. I am thankful to You; You should be thankful to me." Hypocrite! That is false spirituality.

True spirituality is manifested in a spirit of being poor in spirit. Why poor in spirit? Because he has seen the Lord. If you have seen the Lord, how rich, how full He is, you realize how wretched, how poor, how blind, how naked you are. Even when Daniel, the beloved of God, saw the Lord, he said, "My beauty turned into corruption." Only one who has not seen the Lord thinks that he is righteous above all else. When Job saw the Lord, he repented in dust and ashes. Dear brothers and sisters, the one sure mark of true spirituality is being poor in spirit—not pretending to be poor, but *are* poor because you have seen the Lord. The more you see the Lord, the more you realize how poor you are.

Rich In Love

The second mark of true spirituality is being rich in love. Knowledge puffs up, but love builds up. We may have mental knowledge, even mental knowledge concerning the Scripture; we may know the doctrines. Darby said high intellectual understanding of the doctrines of the Scripture only puffs us up. It is pseudo-spirituality, but love builds up. True spiritual knowledge produces love.

In Paul's prayer in Ephesians, he prayed that we may be granted the spirit of wisdom and understanding to the full knowledge of God. Then he followed this prayer with another prayer—that our spirit may be strengthened by the Holy Spirit, that Christ may dwell in our hearts, that we may apprehend with all the saints the length and breadth, the width and height of the love of God which passes knowledge. Dear brothers and sisters, real knowledge brings in love, love to God and love to the brethren. So, true spirituality is expressed in love because God is love. It is not expressed in knowledge only but is expressed in love. That is the real thing.

The Sentence Of Death

The third mark of spirituality is the sentence of death. In Galatians 6, Paul said, "I have the brands of Christ upon me, the wounds of Christ." Dear brothers and sisters, are we intact, never having been dealt with? Have we never been poured from one vessel to another vessel? Does our flavor remain the same? If we have been dealt with by the Lord, there will be the sentence of death upon us. We dare not trust in ourselves; we dare not raise our heads and, yet, we know the resurrection power of the life of our Lord. That is the true mark of spirituality.

Seeing The Heart Of God

Fourth, true spirituality is marked by visions and revelations. Now by that I do not mean what people say today: "Well, I had a vision, I had a dream; I had a revelation." What I mean is, he who is spiritual is so pure in his heart that he sees God. He sees the very heart of God, the very mind of God, the very purpose of God. He is the enlightened one. He walks in the light as God is in the light and in fellowship with the other

brethren and the blood of Jesus Christ cleanses
him from all his sins.

Spiritual Discernment

The fifth mark of true spirituality is that the
spiritual   discerns   all   things.   Spiritual
discernment comes through much experience
and many dealings with the Lord. It is because
you become transparent, and as you become
transparent, everything comes through. When
the Lord Jesus was on earth, He did not need
people to tell Him about man because He knew,
He saw through and through. He looked at Peter,
and Peter withered. The spiritual discerns all
things; he is not cheated by appearance; he can
see through.

Spiritual discernment is not for judgment, it
is for ministry. Our problem is, the more we see,
the more we judge. We become the judge in the
supreme court. We judge everybody, everything,
but true spirituality gives you discernment in
order that you may serve. How can you serve
your brothers and sisters if you cannot discern?
You do not know where they are, what their
spiritual condition is. They may say one thing,

but they are not. Oftentimes, we say it, but we are not what we say. You need discernment; it is for service, for ministry. But unfortunately, another mark of the spiritual is, he is discerned of no one. In other words, he will be misunderstood by everybody. That is the price you have to pay.

So, dear brothers and sisters, when we sing the song "Maranatha," it touches me very deeply. The Lord is coming soon. I do believe that we do have the desire to see Him, but I was thinking, when I see Him, how much is of Him? How much can He receive back to Himself? How much will be burned? How many days, months, or years have I lived under deception, thinking that I have it but it is a counterfeit, it is a pretense, it is not real; it is not Christ in me, it is me trying to be like Christ? I really feel fearful. That is the reason why we feel burdened. These are not days when we can play around anymore, playing with our spiritual life, playing with church life; we do not have time for that. My prayer is, the earlier we realize how much is not real, the better, that we may allow the Spirit of God to really bring Christ into our lives; then when we see Him, as Paul said, we shall not be ashamed. May the Lord help us.

Let us pray:

Lord, we may talk about spirituality. We may take up the terminology and try to appear spiritual. Forbid it! We pray that we may all fall at Thy feet, allow Thee to examine us, to prove us. Lord, whatever cost it may be, if it means that we will be reduced to zero, Lord, do it. We pray that, from now on, it is Christ in us, the hope of glory. In the name of our Lord Jesus. Amen.

QUESTION AND ANSWER

Q: Is there a significant difference between the heart and the spirit? If there is a difference, how does the heart influence our spiritual life?

There is a difference between the heart and the spirit, but first of all, let me say this: Even though we can see the distinction between the heart and the spirit, yet, they are so intertwined, you really cannot separate them completely. As our physical heart is the center of our physical being, so our heart is the center of our moral being. The human spirit was created by God. It became dead through sin, and it is brought into new life by the Holy Spirit. We know our spirit by its functions, its faculties. In a sense, our spirit is an organ, and it is known by its faculties. We know that in our spirit there is communion. God is Spirit, and *only* spirit can communicate with Spirit. That is why God created us with a spirit, that we may commune with Him, and out of such communion comes worship.

We also know from the word of God that one of the faculties of our spirit is conscience. The Bible tells us that the conscience sometimes constrains us and sometimes restrains us. Sometimes, it gives its approval and, sometimes, it condemns us. So, the functioning of our conscience results in our walk. How do we walk before God?

Then also from the word of God, we find that our spirit has the function of intuition, that is, direct knowledge. It is not knowledge that comes from the outside through information, but it is a direct knowledge that comes from God. Intuitively, we know the mind of God, the will of God. This has much to do with our service, our ministry unto the Lord.

What is the heart? The heart, as we learn from the word of God, actually is the passage between the spirit and the soul. In the heart, there is the conscience of the spirit. "Let us approach with a true heart, in full assurance of faith, sprinkled as to our hearts from a wicked conscience" (Hebrews 10:22). We find that conscience is part of the heart and, yet, we find that the heart also includes all the faculties of the soul.

For the word of God is living and operative, and sharper than any two-edged sword, and penetrating to the division of soul and spirit, both of joints and marrow, and a discerner of the thoughts and intents of the heart. (Hebrews 4:12)

Now, the thoughts of the heart have something to do with the mind of the soul. The intents of the heart have something to do with the volition, the will of the soul. So, the heart includes both the mind, the intellect, and the will, the volition of the soul. Of course, in the heart, you also have the emotion of the soul. For instance, in Hebrews 3:7-8a, it says, "Wherefore, even as says the Holy Spirit, To-day if ye will hear his voice, harden not your hearts." That has something to do with our emotions. So the heart, actually, is the connection and the passageway between the spirit and the soul.

One verse in the Scriptures that is very basic to the meaning of the heart is Proverbs 4:23: "Keep thy heart more than anything that is guarded; for out of it are the issues of life." Out of the heart are the issues of life. Our heart has much to do with our spiritual life, because when we hear the gospel, the word is as a seed. It falls upon our heart. So as you read the parable of the sower in Matthew 13, the sower goes out to sow the seed. The seed falls upon hearts. Some hearts are ready, some hearts are not ready; and the seed has to fall into good ground, a readied heart. When the gospel is preached, usually, it touches the conscience of our heart. When the conscience of our heart is touched, it brings in conviction and repentance and that is how life enters into us. In the same way, you find life comes out of us. Out of the heart come forth all the issues of life.

When we believe in the Lord Jesus, our spirit is renewed. Now, who comes to dwell in our spirit? The Holy Spirit. Christ comes to dwell in our spirit by the Holy Spirit. So, God actually dwells in our spirit. That is the holiest of all. But this is the beginning of spiritual life. What is the growth of spiritual life? It is that Christ who dwells in our spirit comes forth and begins to dwell in our heart. That is spiritual growth.

In the prayer of the apostle Paul in Ephesians 3:16, he said, "That he may give you according to the riches of his glory, to be strengthened with power by his Spirit in the inner man." The inner man is the spirit; and when our spirit is strengthened by the Holy Spirit: "that the Christ may dwell, through faith, in your hearts." It is as if when our spirit is strengthened by the Holy Spirit that Christ begins to come from the spirit through the heart into the heart and dwell in the heart. He begins to displace self, who used to dwell in the soul, and now He comes and dwells in our heart. He is able to express Himself through all the faculties of our heart: the conscience, the mind, the will, and the emotion.

In a very real sense, we find that the heart is a key to our spiritual life. That is why we need to guard our heart more than anything else lest our heart become cold, lest our heart become hardened or darkened; because if that is the case, our spiritual life begins to fade. That is the difference between the heart and the spirit. Again, I say, you really cannot separate them because they are all together.

Q: Will you please explain how our soul or an evil spirit can invade our spirit?

Remember that our spirit is an organ just as our soul is an organ. Let me put it this way: The holiest of all is just a room. It is empty until you move the ark into that room, and then the glory of God will fill that room. So, our spirit is like the holiest of all of our being—an organ, a room. It will be empty if nobody dwells there, but thank God that He comes and dwells in our spirit by the Holy Spirit. So, the Holy Spirit should be the life of our spirit. That is what God ordained it to be. The Holy Spirit is to be the life of our spirit.

Now, the soul is also an organ. Who dwells there? You dwell there; I dwell there; self dwells there. Self is in control and expresses itself through all the faculties of the soul. If our spirit is not in communion with the Holy Spirit, or if our spirit is not cooperating with the Holy Spirit, then it leaves the door wide open for what is outside to invade the spirit. To put it more technically, it is really not the soul that invades the spirit, it is the soul-life that invades the spirit. If our spirit is not under the control of the

Holy Spirit, then our self, the flesh is able to penetrate into our spirit and pollute it. The result is, even if something comes out of the spirit, yet, it is not the right spirit. Sometimes, it expresses our flesh, our own person; at other times, even the evil spirit can enter into it.

The best illustration we find in the Bible is in Luke 9. Our Lord Jesus was on His way from Galilee to Jerusalem, and He passed by the villages of Samaria. There was such hostility between the Samaritans and the Jews, and because our Lord's face was towards Jerusalem, the Samaritans would not receive Him. The two Sons of Thunder, John and James, came to the Lord and said, "Lord, they should never do such a thing to You. How dare they not receive You! They need to be punished. Let us call down fire from heaven and burn them up. That is what they deserve." Remember that our Lord Jesus said, "You do not know what kind of a spirit you have." At that time, the Lord went to Jerusalem in the spirit of a Lamb, but here you find the disciples were of a different spirit. It is true, they respected the Lord so much, but it was not from God, it was from the flesh. It came from the emotion of the soul. They were emotionally stirred and lost the quietness of the spirit. So, here is an illustration of how the soul-life can penetrate and pollute the spirit.

Now, maybe I should say this: How do we know it is the spirit and not just the soul? Our soul is in the body; our body is the shell and our soul is in the body and our spirit is in the soul. The soul is the shell of the spirit. The greatest problem with our Christian life is that the shell of our soul is so hard that it imprisons our spirit and will not let the spirit come forth. That is our real problem. Even though we are saved and we have Christ in our spirit, Christ cannot come out because our soul is so strong, it just imprisons Christ. There is no breakthrough, and that is why, for the release of the spirit, you need the breaking of the outward man. Really, that is the most important, basic part. We need the breaking of the outward man, which speaks of the soul and the body, and the release of the inward man, that is, the spirit. That work can only be done by the cross. The Holy Spirit will apply the cross to our lives to break the outward man, to release the inward man. Actually, that is the most basic problem with our Christian life.

Another problem with our Christian life is that the soul and the spirit are so close together that even when the spirit comes out, it comes out together with the soul. That is why, in Hebrews 4, it says there needs to be a dividing of the spirit and the soul. The dividing is done by the Lord, our High Priest, with the living word; and all we can do is lay on the altar and let Him do it.

Then, there is this matter of how the soul life can penetrate and pollute the spirit. Brothers and sisters, the more we are civilized, the more we grow up, the more we know how to cover up. People cannot really touch your real person. We may be together for years, but our real person has never come forth because we are always on our guard. When does your spirit really come out? When you are not on guard, that is when your spirit comes out, and that shows who you really are and where you are. So, when the spirit comes out, when your real person comes out and it comes out in an ugly way, you know it has been polluted by the soul life. That is why, in II

Corinthians 7:1, it says we need to purify ourselves from the pollution of the flesh and spirit—our spirit can be polluted—so that we may perfect holiness in the fear of God.

Now, as to the evil spirit, we need to remember that when our spirit is dead in sins and transgressions, the organ is still there. So, it is still exposed to the spiritual realm. Even though it has lost its communication with God, its proper environment, yet, it is still open and exposed to the spiritual realm; and in the spiritual realm, you have the evil spirits, too. That is why the unregenerate person can communicate with evil spirits, and the same thing can happen if we are open to the evil spirits. That is the reason why we need to be constantly filled by the Spirit of God. Then the evil spirit has no way to get into our spirit.

Q: Is the invasion of the mind by the evil spirit similar to possession by the evil spirit? How do we keep our mind safe from such invasion?

Now, there is a distinction here. When we talk about possession, it refers to the body. As you study the gospels, you find that the evil spirit possesses the body of a person, and we call that possession. But when the evil spirit penetrates our mind, we do not call it possession because it is not a physical thing. We call it obsession. He can obsess our mind, blind our mind, block our mind, keep our mind in darkness. That is the work of the evil spirit. To be delivered from obsession, you need light, truth. When the truth of God comes as light, it penetrates through our obsession and clears our mind from the influence of the evil spirit.

The way to keep our mind safe from such invasion is to walk in the light. If we walk in the light as God lives in the light, we have fellowship one with another and the blood of God's Son, Jesus Christ, cleanses us from all our sins.

Q: Are we to help any brother or sister who is deceived in his or her own spirituality? If so, how?

In Galatians 6, we are told that those who are spiritual should restore those who are taken in some fault. In other words, we do have a responsibility for one another. Now suppose there is one who is deceived. He thinks he is spiritual but, actually, it is false. Now, how are we going to help such a person? Basically, only God can do such a work. We cannot do anything. For instance, Saul of Tarsus was full of false spirituality. He thought he was serving God; he was very zealous, very orthodox, very traditional. Who could convince him that he was in deception? Nobody could, but God could. When the Lord revealed Himself to this man, he was delivered from false spirituality. He began to see that his past was all false.

The same thing is true with Job of Uz. Job thought he was righteous, and he was. He was so self-righteous, he wanted to argue with God. Who could convince him? Not his friends—it was a vision of God that did the work. Immediately, he repented in dust and ashes. So, in a sense, to be delivered from the deception of false spirituality, you need a visit from God. If God will reveal Himself to that person, it solves it.

After saying this, then let us say we can help our brothers and sisters. In what way? If we live in the light, our light will shine upon those who are in darkness and bring them under conviction and into deliverance. Sometimes, you feel you are all right, but if you come into the presence of one who really walks with God, even without words, the light shines upon you and you are convicted. So, that is the way to help.

Q: If we long for the Lord's appearing and, yet, there is a sense in our soul that we are not ready, how is that inconsistency resolved in us, in our soul? How can we sing a song like "Maranatha" without feeling hypocritical?

Spiritual life is a paradox. I think we need to remember that. On the one hand, in your spirit, you do long to see Him face to face. You are not satisfied just knowing that He is with you in the spirit. You want to see Him face to face. If you love the Lord, you long for His return. Whether you are ready or not, that is not the question; it is He that you long for. Even if I am not ready, I hope my unreadiness will not prevent Him from coming. We need to love Him in that selfless way, if I may put it this way, and not selfishly say, "Lord, don't come, I am not ready yet." On the other hand, you really feel that you are never ready. He is just too good for you, and if you feel you are ready, you are not ready. But if you feel

75

that you are not ready, that urges you to pursue Him more. So in I John, it says:

Beloved, now are we children of God, and what we shall be has not yet been manifested; we know that if it is manifested we shall be like him, for we shall see him as he is. And every one that has this hope in him purifies himself, even as he is pure. (I John 3:2-3)

This longing for His return actually purifies us. It makes us ready. So, it is a paradox, but thank God that we do live in such a paradox.

Other Books Printed By
Christian Testimony Ministry

WHY DO WE SO GATHER?
WORSHIP

LANCE LAMBERT

CALLED UNTO HIS ETERNAL GLORY
GOD'S ETERNAL PURPOSE
IN THE DAY OF THY POWER
JACOB I HAVE LOVED
LIVING FAITH
LESSONS FROM THE LIFE OF MOSES
LOVE DIVINE
MY HOUSE SHALL BE A HOUSE OF PRAYER
PREPARATION FOR THE COMING OF THE LORD
REIGNING WITH CHRIST
SPIRITUAL CHARACTER
THE GOSPEL OF THE KINGDOM
THE IMPORTANCE OF COVERING
THE LAST DAYS AND GOD'S PRIORITIES
THE PRIZE
THE SUPREMACY OF JESUS CHRIST
THINE IS THE POWER!
THOU ART MINE

T. AUSTIN-SPARKS

THE LORD'S TESTIMONY AND THE WORLD NEED

HARVEY CEDARS CONFERENCE

STEPHEN KAUNG

HEAVENLY VISION
SPIRITUAL RESPONSIBILITY

CONGDON, HILE, KAUNG

SPIRITUAL MINISTRY
SPIRITUAL AUTHORITY
SPIRITUAL HOUSE
SPIRITUAL SUBMISSION

STEPHEN KAUNG

SPIRITUAL KNOWLEDGE
SPIRITUAL POWER
SPIRITUAL REALITY
SPIRITUAL VALUE
SPIRITUAL BLESSING
SPIRITUAL DISCERNMENT